If found please return to these
lovers...

_____

Introduction

It wasn't until I had my bachelorette party
that I realised just how little I knew about
my husband. Don't get me wrong. We didn't rush
 into marriage or anything but there were
 little things I didn't know. Little things
 like his favourite song or whether he had
                stitches as a kid.

 Those little details about a person define
them. They're fun to know. They're important.
This book is dedicated to the little things.

Have fun with the writing prompts, quizzes and
         the truth or dare challenges.

I'd love to see how you go! Please share your
       photos on Instagram @30everafter.

Describe your partner

My partner is…

Partner a: Circle all the words that describe your partner

Caring	Genuine	Energetic
Patient	Loyal	Wise
Kind	Calm	Reliable
Compassionate	Sexy	Cute
Charming	Funny	Witty
Peaceful	Chivalrous	Humble
Lovable	Honest	Resourceful
Responsible	Romantic	Gentle
Decisive	Strong	Confident
Shy	Passionate	Reflective
Creative	Dramatic	Cheerful
Attractive	Fun loving	Friendly

My partner is...

Partner b: Circle all the words that describe your partner

Caring	Genuine	Energetic
Patient	Loyal	Wise
Kind	Calm	Reliable
Compassionate	Sexy	Cute
Charming	Funny	Witty
Peaceful	Chivalrous	Humble
Lovable	Honest	Resourceful
Responsible	Romantic	Gentle
Decisive	Strong	Confident
Shy	Passionate	Reflective
Creative	Dramatic	Cheerful
Attractive	Fun loving	Friendly

How well do you
know your partner?

Firsts & Lasts

Take turns asking the questions below.

Place a check mark for every question answered right and a 'x' for every incorrect answer.

A: What was your partner wearing on your first date?

B: What was your partner wearing on your first date?

A: Where did you go on your first date?

B: Where did you go on your first date?

A: Where did we have our first kiss?

B: Where did we have our first kiss?

Firsts & Lasts

Take turns asking the questions below.

Place a check mark for every question answered right and a 'x' for every incorrect answer.

A: When was the last time you saw your partner cry?

B: When was the last time you saw your partner cry?

A: When was the last time you both had a good night's rest?

B: When was the last time you both had a good night's rest?

A: When was the last time you had a good passionate kiss?

B: When was the last time you had a good passionate kiss?

Have you ever...

Take turns asking the questions below.

Place a check mark for every question answered right and a 'x' for every incorrect answer.

A: Has your partner ever gone skinny dipping? ◯

B: Has your partner ever gone skinny dipping? ◯

A: Has your partner ever broken a bone? ◯

B: Has your partner ever broken a bone? ◯

A: Has your partner ever won a contest? ◯

B: Has your partner ever won a contest? ◯

Have you ever...

Take turns asking the questions below.

Place a check mark for every question answered right and a 'x' for every incorrect answer.

A: Has your partner ever been caught watching porn? ◯

B: Has your partner ever been caught watching porn? ◯

A: Has your partner ever been to a strip club? ◯

B: Has your partner ever been to a strip club? ◯

A: Has your partner ever sat in a cop car? ◯

B: Has your partner ever sat in a cop car? ◯

Movies

Take turns asking the questions below.

Place a check mark for every question answered right and a 'x' for every incorrect answer.

A: What's your partner's favourite movie?   ◯

B: What's your partner's favourite movie?   ◯

A: What's one movie your partner can watch over and over again?   ◯

B: What's one movie your partner can watch over and over again?   ◯

A: What is one movie your partner can't stand?   ◯

B: What is one movie your partner can't stand?   ◯

Favourite things...

Place a check mark for every question answered right and a 'x' for every incorrect answer.

A: What's one thing your partner must take when traveling?

B: What's one thing your partner must take when traveling?

A: What song/album does he/she like to play when driving?

B: What song/album does he/she like to play when driving?

A: What thing would your partner save from a burning house?

B: What thing would your partner save from a burning house?

Favourite things...

Take turns asking the questions below.

Place a check mark for every question answered right and a 'x' for every incorrect answer.

A: What are 3 things your partner can't live without?	◯
B: What are 3 things your partner can't live without?	◯
A: Did your partner have a favourite toy growing up?	◯
B: Did your partner have a favourite toy growing up?	◯
A: What's one thing your partner should get rid of?	◯
B: What's one thing your partner should get rid of?	◯

Millionaire...

Take turns asking the questions below.

Place a check mark for every question answered right and a 'x' for every incorrect answer.

A: What's one thing your partner would buy with one million dollars?

B: What's one thing your partner would buy with one million dollars?

A: Would your partner still work after winning one million dollars?

B: Would your partner still work after winning one million dollars?

A: Who would your partner tell first if they won the lottery (besides you)?

B: Who would your partner tell first if they won the lottery (besides you)?

Hall passes...

Take turns asking the questions below.

Place a check mark for every question answered right and a 'x' for every incorrect answer.

A: Who are your partner's hall passes?

B: A: Who are your partner's hall passes?

A: Which celebrity would your partner kiss, shag and marry?

B: Which celebrity would your partner kiss, shag and marry?

A: Who was your partner's first celebrity crush?

B: Who was your partner's first celebrity crush?

Childhood memories...

Take turns asking the questions below.

Place a check mark for every question answered right and a 'x' for every incorrect answer.

A: What's your partner's favourite childhood past time?

B: What's your partner's favourite childhood past time?

A: What was your partner's favourite sport?

B: What was your partner's favourite sport?

A: Did your partner have imaginary friends as a child?

B: Did your partner have imaginary friends as a child?

Around the world...

Take turns asking the questions below.

Place a check mark for every question answered right and a 'x' for every incorrect answer.

A: What's one place your partner wants to travel to? ◯

B: What's one place your partner wants to travel to? ◯

A: Where is your partner's favourite place in the world? ◯

B: Where is your partner's favourite place in the world? ◯

A: How many languages does your partner speak? ◯

B: How many languages does your partner speak? ◯

Fill in
the blanks

Intimate moments...

Take turns filling in the blank

Partner A: I knew we had something
            special when...

Partner B: I knew we had something
            special when...

Intimate moments...

Take turns filling in the blank

Partner A: When we had our first
kiss, I felt…

Partner B: When we had our first kiss,
I felt…

Intimate moments...

Take turns filling in the blank

Partner A: In 5 years, I'd like
for us to...

Partner B: In 5 years, I'd like for us
to...

Intimate moments...

Take turns filling in the blank

Partner A: I love it when you...

Partner B: I love it when you...

Intimate moments...

Take turns filling in the blank

Partner A: You make me feel the
most loved when...

Partner B: You make me feel the most
loved when...

Intimate moments...

Take turns filling in the blank

Partner A: Something I've always
wanted to do with you is…

Partner B: Something I've always
wanted to do with you is…

Intimate moments...

Take turns filling in the blank

Partner A: I love your
[INSERT FAVOURITE BODY PART]

Partner B: I love your
[INSERT FAVOURITE BODY PART]

Intimate moments...

Take turns filling in the blank

Partner A: My favourite outfit on
you is...

Partner B: My favourite outfit on you
is...

Intimate moments...

Take turns filling in the blank

Partner A: The moment I knew I
loved you was when...

Partner B: The moment I knew I loved
you was when...

Intimate moments...

Take turns filling in the blank

Partner A: If the world ended
tomorrow, I'd tell you...

Partner B: If the world ended
tomorrow, I'd tell you...

Quiz

Quiz:
How well do you
know your partner?

Partner A asks Partner B.

Partner B gets 1 point for every correct answer.

1. What makes me smile?
2. What's my favourite piece of clothing?
3. What is my favourite karaoke tune?
4. Who is my best friend?
5. What's my biggest fear?
6. What's my favourite childhood memory?
7. Who was my childhood best friend?
8. Who was my first love?
9. How many times has my heart been broken?
10. What weird quirk do I have?
11. Did I ever have braces?
12. Have I ever been to the hospital?
13. Was I a straight A student in school?
14. Where in the world have I travelled?
15. What's number one on my bucket list?
16. Who do I admire the most?
17. If money were no object, what would I be
    doing right now?
18. What has been my biggest regret to date?
19. What is one movie I can watch over and over
    again?
20. What's my favourite sport?
21. When was the last time I cried?
22. What was I wearing yesterday?
23. What's my favourite holiday?
24. How many siblings do I have?
25. What's my favourite colour?

Quiz:
How well do you
know your partner?

1. What makes me smile?
2. What's my favourite piece of clothing?
3. What is my favourite karaoke tune?
4. Who is my best friend?
5. What's my biggest fear?
6. What's my favourite childhood memory?
7. Who was my childhood best friend?
8. Who was my first love?
9. How many times has my heart been broken?
10. What weird quirk do I have?
11. Did I ever have braces?
12. Have I ever been to the hospital?
13. Was I a straight A student in school?
14. Where in the world have I travelled?
15. What's number one on my bucket list?
16. Who do I admire the most?
17. If money were no object, what would I be doing right now?
18. What has been my biggest regret to date?
19. What is one movie I can watch over and over again?
20. What's my favourite sport?
21. When was the last time I cried?
22. What was I wearing yesterday?
23. What's my favourite holiday?
24. How many siblings do I have?
25. What's my favourite colour?

Questions

Questions that bring you closer

1.   When do you feel the most appreciated in our relationship?

2.   What's something I do that makes you feel like a king/queen?

3.   What's one challenge we've had to overcome?

4.   Do you think there's a difference between loving someone and being in love with someone?

5.   How do you think we deal with conflict as a couple?

6.   Tell me about a dream you had growing up. What kind of person did you want to become?

7.   Has anything stopped you from pursuing your dreams? If so, what is it?

ions about your day to day

1. Do you think our housework is divided evenly?

2. Do you feel like I should do more to contribute to the household?

3. Who did the housework when you were growing up?

4. How would you feel about getting a cleaner to help us once a week?

5. Are there chores you like doing more than others?

6. What do you think we can do to reduce the amount of housework?

7. If you could skip housework for the week, how would you use your spare time?

Questions about emergencies

1.   If there was a natural disaster and we were both at work or apart, where do you want to meet?

2.   If our state was in a state of emergency, would you want to stay put or leave the city ASAP?

3.   Do you have any survival skills? If so, what are they?

4.   What's the most valuable survival skill you have?

5.   Do you know First Aid?

6.   How do you feel about creating an emergency kit for our family?

7.   If we had to leave our home and you weren't home, what would you like me to take for you?

Questions about finances

1. On a scale of 1-10, how good are you at managing finances?

2. Which one of us is better at managing finances?

3. Are you happy with our financial situation?

4. Do you stress about our finances? When?

5. Growing up, how did your family handle finances?

6. How much money would you like to retire with?

7. How much in lottery money would we need to win for you to quit your job?

Questions about love lessons

1. When did you learn your first lesson in love?

2. What is one experience that's influenced the way you show up in your relationships?

3. What advice would you give the younger generation dating in a world of online sites and dating apps?

4. What's one lesson that you've had to learn a few times before finally getting it right?

5. What did your parents teach you about love?

6. When it comes to love, name one couple you look up to?

7. What's your relationship 'mantra'?

Love notes

Love notes

Tell your partner about a time when you felt vulnerable...

_____

_____

_____

_____

_____

_____

_____

_____

_____

_____

_____

_____

_____

_____

Love notes

Tell your partner about a time when you had to be extra brave?

_____

_____

_____

_____

_____

_____

_____

_____

_____

_____

_____

_____

_____

_____

_____

_____

Love notes

Tell your partner about a time when had to do something
that made you feel uncomfortable…

_____

_____

_____

_____

_____

_____

_____

_____

_____

_____

_____

_____

_____

_____

Love notes

Tell your partner about your first childhood crush

Love notes

Tell your partner about your dream life...

_____

_____

_____

_____

_____

_____

_____

_____

_____

_____

_____

_____

_____

_____

_____

Love notes

Tell your partner about the four famous people you'd like to have dinner with

Love notes

Tell your partner about something that makes you laugh

_____

_____

_____

_____

_____

_____

_____

_____

_____

_____

_____

_____

_____

_____

Love notes

Tell your partner about your happiest memory

_____

_____

_____

_____

_____

_____

_____

_____

_____

_____

_____

_____

_____

_____

_____

_____

Love notes

Tell your partner about something you fear

_____

_____

_____

_____

_____

_____

_____

_____

_____

_____

_____

_____

_____

_____

_____

Love notes

Tell your partner about a tough time in your life

_____

_____

_____

_____

_____

_____

_____

_____

_____

_____

_____

_____

_____

_____

What if…

Songs & Movies

Take turns asking the questions below.

A: If our relationship was a song, which would it be?

B: If our relationship was a song, which would it be?

A: If we were a TV couple, who would we be?

B: If we were a TV couple, who would we be?

A: Which celebrity would play you in a movie?

B: Which celebrity would play you in a movie?

If the world ends...

Take turns asking the questions below.

A: If the economy was obsolete, what survival skills would you have?

B: If the economy was obsolete, what survival skills would you have?

A: Do you believe in doomsday prepping?

B: Do you believe in doomsday prepping?

A: If we were attacked by zombies, would you know what to do?

B: If we were attacked by zombies, would you know what to do?

Spirit animals

Take turns asking the questions below.

A: If you could come back in another life as an animal, which would you be?

B: If you could come back in another life as an animal, which would you be?

A: What is your spirit animal?

B: What is your spirit animal?

A: What's your favourite animal?

B: What's your favourite animal?

Space travel

Take turns asking the questions below.

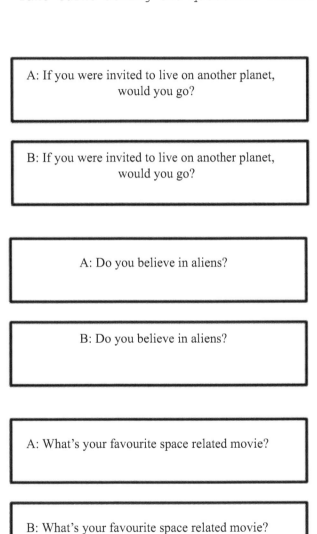

A: If you were invited to live on another planet, would you go?

B: If you were invited to live on another planet, would you go?

A: Do you believe in aliens?

B: Do you believe in aliens?

A: What's your favourite space related movie?

B: What's your favourite space related movie?

100
Date night ideas

Date ideas

1 Go to your local animal shelter and walk some dogs

2 Go to the flea market and buy each other a gif

3 Take a trip to Ikea

4 Pack a picnic and go to the park

5 Have a coffee date at the zoo

6 Pick a scary movie and watch it together

7 Plan your next travel adventure

8 Walk a friend's dog together

9 Borrow a cookbook and cook an exotic meal together

10 Take a workout class together

11 Explore a national park

12 Take a cooking class

13 Go skydiving

14 Head to an amusement park

15 Have a karaoke session right at home

16 Have a dance off

Date ideas

17	Pick a cafe in a busy spot and people watch
18	Work on a DIY project
19	Go camping
20	Rent an Air BnB with no reception
21	Go horseback riding
22	Go on a ferris wheel
23	Eat a dessert only dinner
24	Bake something together
25	Head to the gym together
26	Take a walk on the beach
27	Buy some lottery tickets and imagine what you'd do with the money together
28	Watch the sunrise together
29	Watch a movie at the drive-in
30	Play a game of truth or dare
31	Fine a rooftop and enjoy the city view
32	Go wine tasting

Date ideas

33	Play a game of hide and seek
34	Have a nerf gun fight
35	Go kayaking together
36	Play some boardgames
37	Learn something new together
38	Go to an improvisation acting class
39	Play a game of charades
40	Be tourists in your own city
41	Make something for each other
42	Go axe throwing or glass smashing (yep it exists!)
43	Take a boxing class together
44	Show each other your favourite spots in the city
45	Do a puzzle together
46	Go fruit picking
47	Play frisbee
48	Go on a scavenger hunt

Date ideas

49	Make a bucket list
50	Do a cross word puzzle
51	Go to open houses
52	Go for a drive to the country
53	Take a painting class
54	Go to an escape room
55	Go bowling
56	Play laser tag
57	Go to a poetry reading
58	Visit a cat cafe
59	Go to an art gallery
60	Pick a TV show and binge on Netflix
61	Host your own movie marathon
62	Lie in bed all day and watch movies
63	Go roller or ice skating
64	Go swimming

Date ideas

65	Learn how to skateboard
66	Fly a kite
67	Draw your own comic
68	Write your own love story
69	Go to a painting class
70	Paint each other a picture
71	Take a photography class
72	Take photos of each other
73	Play dress up
74	Feed each other a meal without utensils
75	Blindfold each other and play guess the food
76	Go shopping for a new outfit
77	Have a rooftop picnic
78	Go stargazing
79	Go to a comedy show
80	Go to a dog park

Date ideas

81	Visit your favourite bookstore
82	Watch a sports game
83	Go to a concert
84	Go to an open mic night
85	Grab brunch together
86	Take a ferry ride
87	Rent bikes and ride around the city
88	Go to a carnival
89	Make your own carnival games
90	Go for a late night swim
91	Head to the aquarium
92	Play mini golf
93	Head to the arcade
94	Play strip poker
95	Play Pictionary
96	See a burlesque show

Date ideas

97	Rent a boat for the day
98	See an astrologer together
99	Have your tarot cards read
100	Race go-karts

100 things I
love about you

Partner A writes:
100 things I love about you

1

2

3

4

5

6

7

8

9

10

11

12

13

14

15

16

Partner A writes:
100 things I love about you

17 _____

18 _____

19 _____

20 _____

21 _____

22 _____

23 _____

24 _____

25 _____

26 _____

27 _____

28 _____

29 _____

30 _____

31 _____

32 _____

Partner A writes:
100 things I love about you

33 _____

34 _____

35 _____

36 _____

37 _____

38 _____

39 _____

40 _____

41 _____

42 _____

43 _____

44 _____

45 _____

46 _____

47 _____

48 _____

Partner A writes:
100 things I love about you

49

50

51

52

53

54

55

56

57

58

59

60

61

62

63

64

Partner A writes:
100 things I love about you

65 _____

66 _____

67 _____

68 _____

69 _____

70 _____

71 _____

72 _____

73 _____

74 _____

75 _____

76 _____

77 _____

78 _____

79 _____

80 _____

Partner A writes:
100 things I love about you

81

82

83

84

85

86

87

88

89

90

91

92

93

94

95

96

Partner A writes:
100 things I love about you

97

98

99

100

Partner B writes:
100 things I love about you

1

2

3

4

5

6

7

8

9

10

11

12

13

14

15

16

Partner B writes:
100 things I love about you

17 _____

18 _____

19 _____

20 _____

21 _____

22 _____

23 _____

24 _____

25 _____

26 _____

27 _____

28 _____

29 _____

30 _____

31 _____

32 _____

Partner B writes:
100 things I love about you

33 _____

34 _____

35 _____

36 _____

37 _____

38 _____

39 _____

40 _____

41 _____

42 _____

43 _____

44 _____

45 _____

46 _____

47 _____

48 _____

Partner B writes:
100 things I love about you

49 _____

50 _____

51 _____

52 _____

53 _____

54 _____

55 _____

56 _____

57 _____

58 _____

59 _____

60 _____

61 _____

62 _____

63 _____

64 _____

Partner B writes:
100 things I love about you

65 _____

66 _____

67 _____

68 _____

69 _____

70 _____

71 _____

72 _____

73 _____

74 _____

75 _____

76 _____

77 _____

78 _____

79 _____

80 _____

Partner B writes:
100 things I love about you

81

82

83

84

85

86

87

88

89

90

91

92

93

94

95

96

Partner B writes:
100 things I love about you

97

98

99

100

Your monthly
bucket list

Our bucket list

What are we doing?

_____

_____

_____

What do we need to do to make it
happen?

_____

_____

_____

_____

Date we need to do it by:

_____

_____

_____

Our bucket list

What are we doing?

_____

_____

_____

What do we need to do to make it
happen?

_____

_____

_____

_____

Date we need to do it by:

_____

_____

_____

_____

Our bucket list

What are we doing?

_____

_____

_____

What do we need to do to make it happen?

_____

_____

_____

_____

Date we need to do it by:

_____

_____

_____

Our bucket list

What are we doing?

What do we need to do to make it happen?

Date we need to do it by:

Our bucket list

What are we doing?

_____

_____

_____

What do we need to do to make it happen?

_____

_____

_____

_____

Date we need to do it by:

_____

_____

_____

Our bucket list

What are we doing?

_____

_____

_____

What do we need to do to make it happen?

_____

_____

_____

_____

Date we need to do it by:

_____

_____

_____

_____

Our bucket list

What are we doing?

_____

_____

_____

What do we need to do to make it
happen?

_____

_____

_____

_____

Date we need to do it by:

_____

_____

_____

Our bucket list

What are we doing?

_____

_____

_____

What do we need to do to make it
happen?

_____

_____

_____

_____

Date we need to do it by:

_____

_____

_____

_____

Our bucket list

What are we doing?

_____

_____

_____

_____

What do we need to do to make it happen?

_____

_____

_____

_____

Date we need to do it by:

_____

_____

_____

_____

Our bucket list

What are we doing?

What do we need to do to make it happen?

Date we need to do it by:

Our bucket list

What are we doing?

_____

_____

_____

What do we need to do to make it happen?

_____

_____

_____

_____

Date we need to do it by:

_____

_____

_____

Our bucket list

What are we doing?

_____

_____

_____

What do we need to do to make it happen?

_____

_____

_____

_____

Date we need to do it by:

_____

_____

_____

_____

That's all!

If you want more activity books like this and freebies, send me an email at iona@30everafter.com with the subject line: Send me more love.

Made in the USA
San Bernardino, CA
10 May 2020